Teaching Vocabulary Is the Writing Teacher's Job

Teaching Vocabulary Is the Writing Teacher's Job

Why and How

By

Keith S. Folse
University of Central Florida

University of Michigan Press
Ann Arbor

First paperback edition 2023

Published in the United States of America by the
University of Michigan Press

Paperback ISBN: 978-0-472-03953-1
Ebook ISBN: 978-0-472-12569-2

First published September 2020

ACKNOWLEDGMENTS

This work is based on an earlier version that appeared in 2008 as the first chapter in *Writing Myths: Applying Second Language Research to Classroom Teaching*. I would like to thank Joy Reid for her work in shaping that version. I would also like to thank Kelly Sippell, my editor at the University of Michigan Press, for her valuable time and effort on this publication.

I am especially grateful to the hundreds and perhaps thousands of students who have been in my writing classes during my 40 years of teaching ESL, as well as the many writing teachers I have spoken with at conferences or via email. Over the years, these interactions have taught me that good writing involves a great many different things, especially vocabulary.

CONTENTS

1. **INTRODUCTION: IN MY WRITING CLASS** 1

2. **OUR STUDENTS' SERIOUS LEXICAL DILEMMA** 8

3. **VOCABULARY AND ESL READING PROFICIENCY** 11

4. **VOCABULARY AND ESL SPEAKING PROFICIENCY** 13

5. **VOCABULARY AND ESL LISTENING PROFICIENCY** 15

6. **VOCABULARY AND ESL WRITING PROFICIENCY** 17

7. **THE ROLE OF VOCABULARY IN ESL WRITING ASSESSMENT** 21
   - Scoring 21
   - Research Studies 23

8. **WHAT ALL TEACHERS SHOULD DO** 26
   - Teach vocabulary. 26
   - Teach the right vocabulary from the right word list. 27
   - Encourage students to become vocabulary detectives. 28
   - Teach learners how to keep a vocabulary notebook that facilitates multiple retrievals of unknown or newly encountered vocabulary. 30
   - Teach collocations, not just single words. 32
   - Test vocabulary. Hold learners accountable. 33
   - Teach paraphrasing and summarizing. 35
   - Make sure that explicit teaching of vocabulary is included in the writing program from the lowest levels of language proficiency. 35

QUESTIONS FOR REFLECTION 38

REFERENCES 41

1. Introduction: In My Writing Class

Most teachers acknowledge the importance of vocabulary in learning a new language, but relatively few teachers make vocabulary a big part of their own classes, with many simply assuming some other class will cover vocabulary, most likely the reading teacher. Because we know the essential role of vocabulary in good writing, especially academic writing, teaching vocabulary is also the writing teacher's job. The purpose of this book is to explain why and how.

• • •

"WOW...another plagiarized paper," I thought to myself as I graded a set of first drafts of academic research essays. The assignment in this particular case was to write an argumentative essay using information from at least two of three sources that we had read in class. Students had already submitted outlines and received my feedback, and this was their first draft based on my feedback to their outlines.

The problem wasn't that the whole paper was plagiarized. Instead, the problem was that the paper was riddled with multiple examples of vocabulary definitely outside this student's English proficiency range. Though the paper had examples of advanced grammatical structures that were beyond this student's English, most readers would quickly notice the incredible lexical incongruities.

In this paper, as in several other students' papers, certain words or other large chunks of language had clearly been taken—plagiarized—from the original readings and inserted into this student's paper. Three of the abundant examples included:

(a) *if a judge were to consider only these pertinent facts*
(b) *in determining the seriousness of their actions*
(c) *a sharp rise in certain crimes has accompanied this unchecked population growth*

What made me suspicious of these seemingly normal phrases? Language. A writer using these phrases shows a native-like grasp of English grammar and vocabulary, but this paper was submitted by an ESL student with upper-intermediate proficiency, not a native writer.

Many ESL programs classify students in five levels: beginning, lower-intermediate, high-intermediate, advanced, and high-advanced. Another example of ESL leveling is the European Common Framework of Reference, or CEFR, which classifies students in eight levels: beginner, elementary, upper-elementary, lower-intermediate, intermediate, upper-intermediate, advanced, and proficiency.

Knowing this proficiency information and the language that normally associated with each gave me even more reason to believe that it was very unlikely that these examples could be produced by any of the ESL writers in this upper-intermediate class. If you are a seasoned writing teacher who also has read your share of plagiarized papers, then you know that the phrase *very unlikely* is polite teacher code to say "absolutely unquestionably beyond a shadow of a doubt impossible" or, more succinctly, "no way!"

Look at the very advanced structures this writer employs here. They are clearly beyond most ESL writers, let alone one at the upper-intermediate proficiency level.

In (a), we have the use of *be* + infinitive (*were to consider*) as well as the subjunctive mood (*were* instead of *was*). In my 40 years of teaching ESL, I have never seen an ESL writer use *be* + infinitive. It is almost never presented in ESL textbooks, let alone practiced. This structure demonstrates very advanced proficiency of not just English, but rather formal, academic English. The second example with subjunctive mood is an advanced proficiency structure. It is taught in ESL books, but it is surprising to find it in original student writing. (Even native writers misuse subjunctive mood.)

In (b), we see the use of a gerund (*determining*) after the preposition *in*. While it is very common for native writers to use this structure, only the most advanced ESL students use this in their own English. Yes, they can get this correct on a multiple choice grammar exam, but very few actually employ this structure in original writing, which is very different from native writer use.

Finally, in (c), this writer has used two complex noun phrases: *a sharp rise in certain crimes* and *this unchecked population growth*. While longer complex noun phrases are common in native academic writing, most ESL writers and even less competent native writers would probably have opted for a more conversational tone that tends to use simple sentences, such as *Crime is increasing a lot, and this is a big problem* or *The population is growing, and now it is out of control.*

So far, we have talked about grammatical structures that made us suspect plagiarism, but what about vocabulary? While it is true that teachers without some training or expertise in ESL language challenges might not have explicitly noticed these structure disparities, surely the glaring vocabulary discrepancies between what this writer used and what a teacher would expect a certain student to use should be much easier to notice. Most teachers tend to notice words, not structures, but both can sound odd and out of place in an example of plagiarized writing.

If we believe that this excerpt is original writing by the student who submitted this paper, then we have to believe that this writer actually chose to use the adjective *pertinent* (a). However, none of my students is likely to know the word *pertinent*, much less collocate, or combine, it correctly with the noun *facts*.

All my students know the adjective *serious* and maybe the adverb *seriously*, but in all my years of teaching writing, I don't think I have ever had a single student use the noun form *seriousness* (b). In fact, I don't know that I have ever used that word in my own writing.

In (c), I am suspicious of the use of the noun *rise* instead of the more common noun *increase*, the more advanced collocation of *sharp rise* (instead of the more expected *big increase*), the verb *accompany* (not a word that most ESL students use on their own), the less frequent adjective *unchecked*, as well as the advanced collocation *unchecked growth*. This student's lexical prowess with new words and extraordinary collocations seemed to have jumped overnight.

As I got near the end of this student's paper, my frustrated and tired mind was filled with all the examples of outright literary theft from some uncited source. In this class, we had discussed plagiarism and cultural attitudes toward it at length, and I was certain that everyone in the class had understood our discussion. For this reason, I found my anger and frustration growing with each plagiarized phrase that was now jumping off the page.

The next question was how I would handle this case. If this paper had been the final draft of a research paper that we had completed in phases, I would have failed the paper and written "too many examples of plagiarism" across the top and been done. Alternatively, I might have written "Your work?" across the top of the page, followed by "See me, please." However, this was not the final draft.

For this assignment in this writing course, I had had the students work in phases because I was teaching them the process of writing a research paper. In this course, each step was an important part of the whole assignment. Students had submitted an outline, gotten my feedback, and now submitted their first draft. I view this very much as teaching, not testing, and students submitting plagiarized work and being called out for it is part of the teaching process. It is not enjoyable to call writers out for cheating on writing assignments, but it is part of a writing teacher's job.

Yes, as teacher, I certainly could have simply returned the paper with the word PLAGIARIZED emblazed across the top. Instead, on this student's paper and on the original articles, I highlighted with a yellow marker the dozen or so words/phrases that were identical.

Then, in a conference with the student, I showed him the highlighted areas. I asked him directly why he had plagiarized. Genuinely surprised by my question, the student answered, "I didn't want to plagiarize. I understand about paraphrasing, and I really tried to paraphrase, but I just can't say these things in a better way. I think this is the best vocabulary to say this. Whatever I write isn't going to be as good."

The sincerity of this student made me stop to think. He was a good student. He had obviously spent time and effort on this assignment (or I would have just written REDO across the top). His paper was actually rather good—except that he had taken language directly from the articles in more than a few cases. (I'm not justifying his actions, just explaining them.) The more I thought about what he had said about the limits of his vocabulary knowledge, the more I was inclined to agree with him: He couldn't express these ideas better than the original author had.

In fact, that was the problem. In a research writing assignment, the goal is not to copy the original author's information but to use the strategies of paraphrasing, summarizing, and synthesizing (Folse & Pugh, 2020). Each of these strategies is complex and, at least in part, culturally based. Further, each requires more than "using your own words" because, in reporting the ideas of others, precision is essential. Therefore, a paraphrase or summary will almost certainly use some terms—words and phrases—from the original.

For these reasons, even native speakers of English have difficulty writing good academic summaries and paraphrases. For an ESL student who is a competent reader, who can distinguish the hierarchy of main ideas from specific detail, and who can make correct decisions about what material to use, questions still arise: Which original terms should be used and why? And for which can a substitute synonym be used? The answers require (a) full understanding of the words and phrases in the original and (b) knowledge of another set of words and phrases to express those same ideas.

In other words, paraphrasing requires extensive vocabulary knowledge. You need to know not only a lot of vocabulary but also a lot about each word or phrase. The writer of a summary or paraphrase must not only be able to select the most precise original terms to use, but also to express original ideas with alternate but accurate vocabulary at the same level of sophistication as the original. Further, the student writer must be familiar with a wide range of collocations. For instance, how would a non-native speaker (NNS) know that *sharp* collocates with *rise* (e.g., *a sharp rise in crime*) or that we don't say *important circumstances* or *urgent circumstances* but *dire circumstances?*

When I brought up this example in a teacher meeting, the ensuing discussion focused on the role of vocabulary in student writing. I pointed out that ESL students who recognize a phrase in an original text as "advanced English" and therefore native-like to them also understand (as my student has stated) that that phrase is "the best vocabulary to say this."

"In my experience," I added, "what we call plagiarism is probably due more to lexical limitations and desperation than cultural differences or outright cheating." I suggested that since paraphrasing and summarizing were two important objectives in this writing course, the teaching element that was missing was appropriate directed vocabulary instruction, which might then allow for proper paraphrasing and summarizing.

The discussion was diffuse and interspersed with teachers' comments about the need for more grammar training. I tried to counter-argue that students were already getting a lot of grammar instruction either directly through lessons on present perfect tense, or indirectly through teacher-circled errors on students' papers. The reality is that grammar mistakes hardly ever impede comprehension, but lexical errors can certainly do so. For instance, when a student writes, *The last reason of some peoples who oppose death penalty is sometimes peoples innocent are execution,* a native English speaker (NES) can understand the student's meaning without too much effort. The writer's message is transparent despite three common grammatical errors—namely wrong plural form (*peoples* instead of *people*), article omission (*death penalty* instead of *the death penalty*), and incorrect syntax or word order (the adjective *innocent* should come before the noun, not after it).

In contrast, when a NNS writes *The ultimate rational of some peoples who defy death penalty is sometimes peoples innocent are execution,* the message is not at all as transparent. In fact, most NESs would find it necessary to re-read this nebulous second sentence several times, and even then they may still not understand the writer's message. Although the grammar mistakes in the first sentence may hinder comprehension, the writer's message is relatively easy to comprehend; in the second sentence, however, the lexical errors really make the sentence nearly incomprehensible.

The student misspelled *rationale* and wrote *rational,* which are two completely different words, but this essay was listing three reasons for a particular viewpoint, not explaining three rationales, which has a different meaning. My best explanation for this lexical error is that the student most likely consulted a thesaurus to find a more impressive synonym for *reason* when in fact the word *reason* would have been perfectly fine.

Next, the word *ultimate* is wrong. This English learner's native language is Spanish, and the Spanish word *último* means last in English. Here the student used a false cognate. Finally (not *ultimately*!), the student used the word *defy* instead of *oppose*. Both are somewhat semantically similar in that they are negative and indicate being against something or someone, but still, native readers who are not so familiar with ESL language errors have a very hard time with these types of lexical errors.

In summary, it is fair to say that grammatical errors are generally local, so they have small (but incremental) effects on readers, but they rarely blur the writer's intended message. In contrast, lexical errors often present larger, more global problems, creating a sort of domino effect as the reader attempts to use meaning obtained from one incorrect vocabulary item to decipher subsequent unclear words.

An astute quote from Wilkins (1972) aptly summarizes the situation: "While without grammar very little can be conveyed, without vocabulary nothing can be conveyed" (p. 111). Despite this, teachers will continue to focus on grammar, much to the detriment of ESL writers.

In this teacher meeting, I might as well have been talking to the wall. Teachers continue to believe that the biggest problem for ESL writing is grammar. "What about all their grammar mistakes?" said one "They make too many mistakes with grammar," said another. Sigh. Huge sigh.

At lower levels, this may be true, as students are still grappling with English verb tenses and sentence structure. However, at the intermediate level and higher, grammar is no longer the real culprit. By that level, students have had a lot of grammar instruction. They have studied all the verb tenses in English. There is no secret verb tense being withheld until students are in the most advanced ESL class. No, I am convinced that above all, what ESL writers need at these higher levels is explicit attention to vocabulary—through direct teaching and direct learning—along with more writing practice and more reading of appropriate genres.

Near the end of the faculty meeting, one teacher said, "You know, I'm sure that vocabulary is important and all, but is this the writing teacher's job? We have enough to do."

I sighed. Again. The pervasive and harmful myth believed by far too many teachers is that vocabulary is not very important in the quality of student writing and is therefore not the writing teacher's job. When I had a chance to get in a word, I finished with "If you believe that good vocabulary can make your students' papers more academic, accessible, and sophisticated, then yes, it seems to me that it really is our job."

2. Our Students' Serious Lexical Dilemma

As an experienced language teacher and as a very experienced language learner, the importance of vocabulary in mastering a new language is very clear to me. When you are trying to learn a new language, you need vocabulary. Notice the verb that I chose to use here: *need*. My use of such a precise, unequivocal lexical item is altogether intentional. I did not hedge with *might need* or *is suggested* or the like. Let's be clear: to function well in a new language, **you absolutely need vocabulary**.

If you have ever tried to express yourself in a foreign language, then you most likely understand how important vocabulary is. Maybe you can remember a time you were searching for the name of something, like when you were trying to use your basic Spanish to order in a restaurant in Costa Rica. Or, in that same restaurant conversation in Spanish, maybe it was the verb *grill* or the adjective *allergic*. Not knowing just one word can sometimes stop a conversation.

Our ESL students understand their lexical plight. They lack sufficient vocabulary. They need **not only a lot of vocabulary but also a great deal about that vocabulary**, especially for advanced academic writing. Our students face a lexical gap between the vocabulary they know and the vocabulary they need to know to succeed academically (Laufer, 1997; Peters & Webb, 2018).

English learners just do not know enough English vocabulary for their language needs. This impacts their ability to read, write, speak, and listen well in English. Many teachers assume that learners can just use context clues to figure out the words they do not know, but the irony is that you need to know a lot of words to have enough context to allow you to guess the meaning of a new word. However, as Batia Laufer (1997) explains so well in her book chapter "The lexical plight in second language reading: Words you don't know, words you think you know, and words you can't guess," correctly guessing the meaning of a new word is very difficult to accomplish. (Because I consider this chapter to be one of the most well-written research-based works on second language vocabulary, it is always the first reading assignment in my teacher training classes.)

English learners certainly recognize this lexical plight (Laufer, 1997) as a tremendous source of frustration and sometimes despair (Green & Meara, 1995; James, 1996; Leki & Carson, 1994), but how limited is their vocabulary?

One way to observe the magnitude of this lexical dilemma would be to compare the vocabulary knowledge between two groups of students who are similar in age and class. According to Laufer and Yano (2001), the English vocabulary level of high school graduates and university students who have studied English is less than a quarter of that known by their native speaking counterparts. This statement about the observed lexical gap between the two groups is based on data from previous studies of English students in Indonesia, Japan, Oman, and Israel.

While the gap that Laufer and Yano (2001) report is large, we might be able to explain this disparity by looking at differences in the two groups' English exposure. Native speakers are exposed to English all day every day, while non-native speakers are not. Most English learners do not have the same ideal conditions that would allow them to learn English naturally. Learning naturally requires two essential elements: time and amount of appropriate input. Native speakers have years to master their language, and they also have the benefit of massive amounts of input at the right level. Children, for example, spend years interacting with their family members, conversing with their friends, and listening to the television. A native speaker has access to millions of words of English input from both human and non-human sources.

While native speakers develop their English skills over many years, ESL learners simply do not have the luxury of unlimited time, especially those in an academic setting. Many of these EAP (English for Academic Purposes) students need to pass a certain proficiency test such as TOEFL®, IELTS®, or other high stakes assessment fairly quickly, often for university admission. Noted second language vocabulary researcher Tom Cobb (1999) points out this ESL "time crunch" by saying that English learners "typically need to know words measured in thousands, not hundreds, but receive language instruction measured in months, not years" (p. 345). This is unfortunate, but accurate.

This gap in vocabulary knowledge between native speakers and similar non-native speakers is well documented and not so surprising. However, what if we compared students in the same grade in high school or same class in an English program? How much lexical difference might we find?

Alkhofi (2015) examined this very question. He measured the vocabulary levels of 79 students enrolled in an intensive English program at a large university in the U.S. As standard practice in most intensive English programs, the students took a placement test to enter the appropriate level of classes, so we would expect similarities in students' proficiency within a level and within a class.

First, Alkhofi (2015) compared the vocabulary of students in two general proficiency levels (low-intermediate and high-intermediate). Not surprisingly, he found lexical variation between the two proficiency levels, indicating the placement exam was working.

Next, Alkhofi examined lexical variability within individual classes of each proficiency level. While we expect language ability differences between levels and we expect some differences between individuals, we do not normally expect great variation among students who have been placed into the same class. However, that is exactly what this study showed. Alkhofi (2015) found tremendous variation in vocabulary knowledge among classmates, something that was not expected.

In addition, Alkhofi (2015) compared vocabulary knowledge by native language, a factor that should not matter in an objective placement exam as the one that had been used. Many different native language groups were represented in this study, but Alkhofi focused on Spanish-speaking students and Arabic-speaking students because they were the two largest native languages spoken by this particular group of students. Comparing 40 students whose native languages were Spanish or Arabic, he found a tremendous difference in English vocabulary knowledge, with the Spanish speakers knowing much more than the Arabic speakers.

This study is but one of the many showing that our students face a tremendous language challenge due to their limited vocabulary. Adult learners in particular are keenly aware of this very real lexical dilemma. They see the acquisition of vocabulary as the greatest source of their language problems and therefore express a strong desire for vocabulary instruction in end-of-term course evaluations, citing their need for more vocabulary development second only to more opportunities to speak English in class (Folse, 2004).

Most ESL learners appreciate the importance of vocabulary and recognize their limited vocabulary as an obstacle to meeting their goals: "Learners themselves readily admit that they experience considerable difficulty with vocabulary, and...most learners identify the acquisition of vocabulary as their greatest single source of problems" (Meara, 1980, p. 221). The next step is to help teachers to realize how serious our students' lexical plight is and to adjust their instruction to focus much more on L2 vocabulary.

3. Vocabulary and ESL Reading Proficiency

"No text comprehension is possible, either in one's native language or in a foreign language, without understanding the text's vocabulary," according to Laufer (1997). Of the four reading skill—reading, speaking, listening, writing—perhaps the skill most associated with vocabulary knowledge is reading. Not surprisingly, the amount of research on vocabulary and reading for both first language and second language is substantial, and it has some of the oldest research studies.

In fact, the intricate relationship between vocabulary knowledge and reading ability has been examined by numerous researchers in first language studies (Alderson, 1984; Baumann, 2009a, 2009b; Beck et al., 1982; Kameenui et al., 1982) and second language studies (Coady et al., 1993; Haynes, 1993; Hu & Nation, 2000; Huckin & Bloch, 1993; Laufer, 1992, 1997; Laufer & Ravenhorst-Kalovski, 2010; Nation & Coady, 1988).

In a study of 217 ESL students speaking Korean, Japanese, Spanish, Chinese, and 15 other native languages, Qian (2002) conducted a substantial correlation study of the relationship between reading and vocabulary knowledge. Vocabulary size was measured with the Vocabulary Levels Test (Nation, 1983), while vocabulary depth was measured with a version of the Word Associates Test (Read, 1998). Reading comprehension was measured with the reading section of a version of the Test of English as a Foreign Language (TOEFL®). Qian (2002) found a strong and significant correlation between vocabulary depth and reading comprehension, as well as between vocabulary breadth and reading comprehension.

Since this is a book about vocabulary and writing, why would we care about the role of vocabulary in reading proficiency? The short answer is that academic writing tasks, especially at the higher levels, almost always require extensive reading. As learners progress in English proficiency, their writing tasks become more complicated, eventually requiring written reactions to readings and texts. Typical academic assignments such as research papers or reaction papers cannot be completed well if writers have not been able to read original works and grasp the ideas well enough to be able to write about them. Insufficient vocabulary will impede or prevent the type of reading needed for these written assignments. As Huckin and Bloch (1993) point out, "Research has shown that second-language readers rely heavily on vocabulary knowledge, and that a lack of vocabulary knowledge is the largest obstacle for second-language readers to overcome" (p. 154). Unfortunately, the domino effect caused by ESL students' lack of lexical knowledge may result in their inability to complete their written assignments.

4. Vocabulary and ESL Speaking Proficiency

Most of us have found ourselves trying to say something in a foreign language and not being able to do so because we either did not know the word or we could not remember the word for something. Obviously, vocabulary knowledge impacts not just how fluent language learners sound but their ability to get one simple idea across to someone else (Folse, 2006a).

Unlike the other four language skills, speaking is the area that has been least investigated with regard to the possible connection with lexical knowledge (Alkhofi, 2015; Koizumi & In'nami, 2013). Because a great deal of second language acquisition research in the 1990s focused on interaction and negotiation of meaning (Ellis et al., 1994; Pica, 1994), work in that decade often focused on tasks that involved both speaking and listening (Joe, 1995; Joe et al., 1996; Newton, 1995).

Hilton (2008) researched the oral production of 56 non-native speakers of English, French, German, and Italian. Results showed that grammatical knowledge showed a negative correlation with error rate, but lexical knowledge correlated significantly with all fluency measures—words per minutes, mean length of run, percentage of hesitation, and rate of hesitation. These results suggest a strong connection between lexical knowledge and speaking fluency.

Solano (2014) studied the role of vocabulary in adult learners in Colombia. The participants in this qualitative study were 13 adult employees taking a beginning English class at their company. This study explored the importance of learners' attitudes toward speaking in English and how their level of vocabulary knowledge influences their speaking performance. In this study, the researcher noted that learners' speaking ability improved as their vocabulary knowledge increased.

In a study involving 311 Japanese learners of English ranging from basic to intermediate in proficiency level, Koizumi and In'nami (2013) examined the contributions of vocabulary size and depth to speaking proficiency. The researchers found that vocabulary size alone was the strongest contributor to speaking proficiency, suggesting greater vocabulary knowledge was crucial to good speaking ability.

Because this is a book about vocabulary and writing, why would we care about the role of vocabulary in speaking proficiency? In some classes, students may have to participate in group discussions before writing their papers. In courses such as history or political science, university courses may include group discussions, which might provide further practice of vocabulary that students will eventually use in the papers they write for the course. In other classes, students may be required to give oral presentations, and students would need to have ample vocabulary to get their ideas across clearly and accurately. The bottom line is that both scenarios require students to be able to speak English to succeed in the class.

5. Vocabulary and ESL Listening Proficiency

Generally, writing and speaking are viewed as productive language skills, while reading and listening are viewed as passive language skills. In reading and listening, learners are in fact **very** actively involved in the process of attempting to comprehend the input, but these two skills are considered "passive" because learners do not actually produce anything.

Several researchers have conducted studies on the role of vocabulary knowledge in both listening and reading. For example, Mecartty (2000) examined how vocabulary knowledge affected English-speaking students' listening and reading comprehension of Spanish, and found that vocabulary knowledge explained a larger amount of variance in reading than in listening. In researching the role of general and text-specific vocabulary knowledge in Iranian students' English listening and reading ability, Mehrpour and Rahimi (2010) found that text-specific vocabulary had a significant effect on both reading and listening comprehension scores, but there was a stronger effect on reading performance.

Not all studies were of both listening and reading, however. Stæhr (2009) conducted an empirical study that focused on the role of vocabulary knowledge in listening comprehension. In this study of 115 advanced Danish learners of English, both vocabulary depth and breadth correlated significantly with listening comprehension. In fact, half of the variance in listening scores was predicted by lexical knowledge. In this study, how much vocabulary students knew clearly interacted with their listening ability.

In a study of 167 Chinese college learners of English, Matthews and Cheng (2015) examined the relationship between recognition of high-frequency words from speech and L2 listening comprehension. Vocabulary proficiency was measured by recognition of target words from the first, second, or third thousand-word frequency levels based on word family lists from the British National Corpus (BNC) and the Corpus of Contemporary American English (COCA). Multiple regression analysis of the data revealed that recognition of words from the third thousand-word frequency level alone could predict 52 percent of the variance in listening comprehension scores. However, recognition scores for words from the first and second thousand-word frequency ranges did not work nearly as well. According to these findings, learners' ability to recognize less frequent words from speech can strongly predict successful L2 listening comprehension for those students.

Likewise, Atas (2018) conducted an empirical study of the role of vocabulary in listening comprehension. The participants were 33 advanced EFL students. Results showed a significant correlation between English vocabulary knowledge and listening comprehension. In short, the more vocabulary you know, the higher your listening comprehension.

Why does this matter in a writing class? Some writing assignments require students to discuss a topic or an article with other students as part of the information-gathering process in developing content and direction for a paper. Listening and speaking go hand-in-hand in being able to navigate a discussion about a topic or source.

6. Vocabulary and ESL Writing Proficiency

I think if you ask most ESL teachers what is important in ESL writing proficiency, they will mention something like “avoiding errors.” If you ask them what they mean by “errors,” I am fairly certain they will attempt to clarify with “grammar errors.” As the opening scene of this volume indicates, many teachers continue to focus on students’ grammatical errors in their writing.

While it is certainly true that our ESL writers make many errors in their writing, their errors are not limited to just grammar, although these may seem to be the most glaring, especially to teachers who are not familiar with ESL students’ errors yet. As Ferris (2018, 4–5) notes, “L2 writers make more errors and different types of errors than do their L1 peers, and they make distinct lexical, syntactic, and discourse-level (e.g., transitional/connecting devices) choices.”

To be sure, ESL writers do make grammatical errors, such as

- *This battle was fight in 1944*—error with past participle in passive voice construction: *fight* should be the past participle *fought.*
- *During Second World War*—error with article: the definite article *the* is missing.

However, they also make vocabulary errors, such as

- *Movies made before 1990 usually took two hours, but current movies tend to be shorter*—a wrong lexical item: *took* should be *lasted.*
- *The city’s current headache involves the amount of housing available. A committee has been formed to look into this headache. Residents are hoping for a creative solution to this particular headache because it impacts so many people*—repetitive vocabulary: a synonym should be used for *headache*: the second *headache* could be changed to *problem* and the third could be changed to *issue.*

Most teachers are aware of grammar errors, but what about vocabulary in student writing? What role does the level of vocabulary used in an essay play in the quality of student writing?

In an interesting study of 140 essays written by Japanese English learners, Ruegg and colleagues (2011) found that essay raters had a very hard time accurately assessing vocabulary usage in student writing. In fact, their results showed that the grammar in a paper influenced the vocabulary rating in a paper much more than the range, frequency, or accuracy of the vocabulary actually used in an essay. Therefore, teachers' general tendency to comment on the grammar of a paper may in fact include vocabulary usage, even indirectly, because raters are not good at differentiating the two.

What does this study tell us writing teachers? For whatever reasons, we still notice grammar in students' papers more than vocabulary. Ruegg and colleagues (2011) found that many teachers' perception of the lexical usage in a student's writing may be incorrectly influenced by that student's grammar errors. Conversely, a paper that had good sentence structure would also be judged to have good vocabulary usage, when in fact that might not be true. Perhaps this is because the easiest types of errors for any teacher to recognize are grammatical, such as a wrong verb tense (**The United Nations has been established in 1945*), or a missing article (**Scientists cannot identify main reason for this reaction*). Perhaps it is because many writing textbooks and some writing courses have a specific grammar syllabus that is an integral part of the course, while there is no parallel vocabulary syllabus.

A focus on lexical issues in student writing, especially in second language writing, is a relatively new area of investigation. For many reasons, early research related to vocabulary tended to focus on reading. The classic book *Why Johnny Can't Read*, which analyzed in detail the well-known reading problems of many students in the U.S., was published in 1955. At that same time, composition weaknesses, if addressed, were done almost always in relation to correspondingly weak reading skills. The often-cited journal *Reading Research Quarterly* has existed since 1965, while the journal *Second Language Writing* was not published until 1992, almost 30 years later.

Today, we have a great deal more data from many different types of studies on second language writing, including the role of vocabulary in good (and weak) writing. For example, we know that students' vocabulary knowledge can have a substantial impact on their ability to write well in English (Engber, 1995; González, 2017; Laufer & Nation, 1995; Roberts & Cimasko, 2008; Ruegg et al., 2011; Santos, 1988).

In an interesting study of both native and non-native writers of English, González (2017) investigated the extent to which lexical frequency and lexical diversity contribute to writing proficiency scores on academic compositions. Does vocabulary use in writing matter? If so, does the use of frequent or infrequent vocabulary matter? Does the use of a range of different vocabulary items—that is, does lexical diversity—matter (Engber, 1995; Laufer, 1994; Linnarud, 1986)?

In this study, González completed a series of intricate analyses of data collected from 172 essays. These essays were composed by 104 multilingual English learners enrolled in advanced second language writing courses at various intensive English programs and 68 monolingual English-speaking university students in a first-year composition course. Three independent raters evaluated the essays according to the TOEFL® iBT independent writing rubric. Results from a binary logistic regression reveal that lexical diversity has a significantly greater impact on writing score than lexical frequency. Post hoc analyses show that lexical frequency has only a moderate relationship to lexical diversity, suggesting that diversity of mid-frequency vocabulary may be more important to writing proficiency than the use of more sophisticated terms that occur less frequently in everyday language.

What exactly do we mean by the term *mid-frequency vocabulary?* Vocabulary can classified as high-frequency, mid-frequency, and low-frequency. According to Schmitt and Schmitt (2012), high-frequency vocabulary includes the 3,000 most frequently used word families, while low-frequency vocabulary includes word families beyond the 9,000 word family limit. Thus, the 6,000 word families falling within the range of frequency from 3,001 to 9,000 are considered mid-frequency vocabulary.

Implications for practice suggest that it is not enough to simply teach vocabulary words in the second language composition classroom, but that teachers need to guide learners in how to employ these words in a varied manner in their writing. Thus, besides teaching the form and meanings of mid-frequency vocabulary such as *consist, dense, rigorous, sinister, conversely,* and *hypothesis,* teachers need to make sure students are able to use these words in their own original writing. Students also need ample opportunities to practice these words in writing that teachers will see and provide feedback on.

González's (2017) findings clearly demonstrate a connection between students' vocabulary use and how their writing may be perceived by readers and raters. Her research is but one of the many empirical studies showing that vocabulary most definitely plays a critical role in successful writing in a variety of ways.

First, insufficient vocabulary knowledge can limit students' ability to understand the sources they are reading for a written assignment (Hu & Nation, 2000; Laufer, 1997; Laufer & Ravenhorst-Kalovski, 2010). For students attempting to complete written academic assignments, not being able to read well due to lack of vocabulary can be detrimental because they are limited in what they can understand from the reading and subsequently in what they can write about that material.

Second, simple vocabulary can make ideas—and the writers—sound simple. Writing is judged by the level of lexical sophistication. How many different words are used and how they are used can matter greatly in writing (Daller et al., 2003; González, 2017; McNamara et al., 2010).

Third, vocabulary errors make writing sound awkward because words are either misused words or they are not the words that native speakers would use. Lexical errors can confuse readers, and confused readers do not generally have a good impression of the writing or the writer (Lennon, 1996; Llach, 2005).

Fourth, limited vocabulary can impair students' abilities to paraphrase or summarize academic material, two of the most important critical skills in academic writing. In my experience, most teachers do not fully grasp how much vocabulary an ESL writer needs to be able to paraphrase. Paraphrasing requires an **extensive lexical repertoire** (Ashrafzadeh & Nimehchisalem, 2015; Chen, 2019; Choy & Mun, 2012; Na & Nhat, 2017). In addition, paraphrasing requires an **extensive knowledge of appropriate synonyms**, which is especially troublesome if a learner does not know the word well in the first place. Notice that I did not say *synonyms* but rather *appropriate synonyms*. The former requires only a thesaurus, while **the latter requires a tremendous depth of lexical knowledge about multiple synonyms** (Ferris, 1994), so the writer can use the one that matches the nuances of the original word that is being paraphrased. This is often difficult even for native speakers to do, so imagine how incredibly problematic this is for a second language writer.

7. The Role of Vocabulary in ESL Writing Assessment

As a writing teacher, you have probably read hundreds of student papers and given detailed feedback with the hope that your students would incorporate your suggestions and queries into the next draft of their papers. At some point, you also assigned a grade to each paper. The question to be considered here is: what role does vocabulary play in your assessment of student writing?

There are perhaps two general reasons for writing teachers to address vocabulary explicitly, and both involve the assessment of student writing. The first reason is a very real and practical one: scoring. For most writing teachers, vocabulary directly contributes to an essay's overall score. The best proof is the many rubrics made by teachers and by high-stakes assessment administrators that illustrate the extent to which vocabulary figures into the overall score of an essay.

The second reason is that research studies published in L2 writing journals in our field have examined which aspects of an essay are most likely to impact the way readers assess it, particularly vocabulary. As has already been discussed, many of these studies have concluded that the empirical data shows that the level of the vocabulary used in a given student's written work can impact the perceived quality of the writing in that paper. These conclusions indicate that teachers and course materials should do as much as possible to help students grow their vocabulary.

Scoring

How is student writing assessed by many teachers? In years past, it was perhaps common for a writing teacher to assign a grade to a paper with just a few almost cursory comments, such as "B. This paper needs more detail in certain areas." or "C. Lacks support. Some language problems."

Most teachers today would recognize these comments as not the type of instructor comments that are very likely to lead to better student writing. How can anyone's writing improve based on such uninformative feedback?

"Certain areas?" Which ones? "Some language problems?" What kind of problems? And where are these problems in my paper? Students cannot read teachers' minds, so the burden is on writing teachers to make their comments meaningful and clear. For further information on how students react to different types of teacher feedback, see Straub (1997), Tsui and Ng (2000), and Hyland and Hyland (2006).

There are several ways to give better feedback. One solution of course is for the teacher to give detailed feedback directly on the paper. This feedback could be about content or organization or language use and be written right where the teacher sees a problem. The benefits of this action are that the comments can be more specific and the student also knows exactly where the issue is.

An additional solution is to create a rubric. Rubrics can vary from a list of categories— such as content, organization, language use, and mechanics with point values for each—to much more specific information, including detailed descriptions of what a 4 in content means, what a 3 in content means, etc. For more detailed information and suggestions on using rubrics, I highly recommend Chapter 3 in Crusan's *Assessment in the Second Language Writing Classroom* (Crusan, 2010).

Not all teachers use rubrics when scoring student writing, but a great many do. When we examine the categories for points on a rubric for student essays, we very often find a separate category for lexical strength. In cases of essay rubrics that do not have a separate lexical category, we often find a category that indirectly awards points for vocabulary.

We can see the allocated role assigned to vocabulary as reflected in actual rubrics used for scoring. Figure 7.1 illustrates the role that vocabulary plays in the ESL Profile (Jacobs et al., 1981), a rubric that became a template for other ESL writing rubrics that followed.

Similarly, the TOEFL® iBT by Educational Testing Services (ETS) uses a 120-point scale with 30 points each for Reading, Listening, Speaking, and Writing. To receive the highest rating of Advanced (24–30 points) (https://www.ets.org/toefl/test-takers/ibt/scores/understanding), test-takers need a strong control of vocabulary in each of the four skill areas assessed.

In the Writing section, for example, vocabulary is explicitly mentioned. The performance descriptors (https://www.ets.org/s/toefl/pdf/pd-toefl-ibt.pdf) give an Advanced rating to writers who typically "produce clear, well-developed, and well-organized text; ungrammatical, unclear, or unidiomatic use of English is rare" and "express an opinion on a controversial issue,

Scoring	Analytically scored on a 100-point system; still widely used
Categories	Five categories (100 points): 1. Content (30 points) 2. Organization (20 points) 3. Vocabulary (20 points) 4. Language Use (25 points) 5. Mechanics (5 points)
Notes	In this seminal instrument, vocabulary clearly counts 20 percent; however, vocabulary indirectly affects points in other areas because excelling in details, range, and support all depend on knowing more words. 1. Organization points can be gained for using "organizing vocabulary" such as *additionally, a second reason,* and *in conclusion.* 2. Content points are lost if a paper "lacks details" or has "limited range." 3. Organization points are lost in a paper with "limited support."

Figure 7.1 ESL Profile © Rubric (from Jacobs et al., 1981)

and support that opinion with appropriate details and explanations in writing, demonstrating variety and range of vocabulary and grammatical structures." Clearly, vocabulary figures prominently in the Writing section of this exam.

Research Studies

We have seen that rubrics—both those made by teachers and those used in high-stakes exams—often mention vocabulary as one of the criteria in how student writing is scored. Further evidence of the strong role that vocabulary plays in a paper's overall score comes from research studies that surprisingly suggest that raters' perceptions of the vocabulary in an essay can also influence raters' perceptions of other categories and thereby "pull up" or "pull down" an essay's overall score.

Figure 7.2 shows some of the studies that examine the role of vocabulary in how a scorer rates student writing. Notice that not all of the findings are listed for each study; the focus is on the degree to which vocabulary knowledge contributes to the overall score of an essay. The limitations of some of the studies are noted.

Study	Method	Findings
Santos (1988)	178 professors at a U.S. university used a 10-point scale to assess two compositions written by NNSs.	1. Professors considered language more than content. 2. The most serious errors were lexical errors.
Ferris (1994)	28 text variables found in 160 university entrance placement exams (by 40 Arabic, 40 Chinese, 40 Japanese, 40 Spanish) were correlated with holistic scores assigned by three independent raters.	1. The top three variables that could predict holistic scores were all lexical in nature: number of words, synonymy/antonymy, and word length. 2. Higher-proficiency students used a variety of lexical choices. 3. Students can benefit from encouragement in the areas of correct word choice, diversity in lexical/syntactic features, and use of cohesion and cohesive devices.
Engber (1995)	66 placement essays written by intermediate to advanced student in an intensive English program with a variety of different first languages were holistically scored. The overall holistic scores were analyzed for correlation with these four measures of lexical richness: lexical variation, error-free variation, percentage of lexical error, and lexical density.	1. High significant correlations were detected for (a) lexical variation—that is, the ratio of different lexical items to the total number of lexical items in the essay (after adjusting for length)—and (b) lexical variation minus error. 2. Of the four measures, the best correlation with overall holistic score was error-free lexical variation. Thus, a writer's ability to use many words and use them well was a strong predictor of a higher overall essay score.

(Continued)

Study	Method	Findings
Dordick (1996)	289 native-speaking first-year college students read one of 10 versions of an ESL student's paragraph, with each version focusing on a specific error: poor rhetorical style (with no grammatical errors); article use; lexical errors; verb and subject-verb agreement; word order; prepositions; connectors and transitions; mixture of all errors; no errors (i.e., control).	Lexical errors (including inappropriate word choice or word form) and verb-related errors interfered with comprehension the most.
Pizarro (2003)	32 non-ESL trained raters were asked to (1) score holistically three university entrance compositions (representing low, middle, and high proficiency) and comment on the best and worst features of each, as well as (2) rate the severity of six error types in 12 example sentences (two sentences for each error type).	1. Grammar and vocabulary were noted as important as either best or worst aspects of the essays. (Limitation: This deals with only three specific essays not on the same topic.) 2. In the sentence errors, the three that were deemed most severe were grammar, organization, and vocabulary.

Figure 7.2 Empirical Studies of the Role of Vocabulary in ESL Essay Overall Scores

8. What All Teachers Should Do

One of our principal pedagogical questions, therefore, is how learners can overcome their lexical gap as quickly as possible. Though lexical learning can take place through natural exposure (e.g., Pigada & Schmitt, 2006), many more studies have shown that ESL students learn and retain vocabulary more effectively when it is explicitly taught (e.g., Laufer & Shmueli, 1997; Min, 2008; Zimmerman, 1997).

1. Teach vocabulary.

The bottom line is that teachers need to teach a lot more vocabulary. Perhaps the single most important point any reader will take away from this volume is that vocabulary proficiency in student writing matters profoundly. We have seen empirical evidence that the vocabulary a writer uses in an essay influences not just the vocabulary component on a rubric but also the overall score via other components such as content and organization.

Students need to improve their active vocabulary usage to improve their writing, but how can learners overcome their lexical gap as quickly as possible? The two options are **natural exposure with repeated practice over time**, much as native speakers do, and **explicit instruction**, as you and I would do if we were to go study German in Berlin right now for a year.

All of us acquired our native languages through mere exposure to the language, so we know that vocabulary learning can certainly take place through natural exposure (e.g., Pigada & Schmitt, 2006). However, this acquisition was possible because we had the benefits of extensive time and extensive repeated interaction with native speakers. Because these two conditions are simply not possible for many ESL learners, especially those with a family who does not speak English or for EFL learners who are by definition not surrounded by English outside of class, we then move to our second option, **explicit instruction**.

Writing teachers need to readjust their mindset to include vocabulary instruction, practice, and assessment as a necessary component in a writing course. Vocabulary needs to be given as much time in the curriculum as learning about paragraph development and brainstorming essay topics.

Many studies have shown students of English learn and retain vocabulary more effectively when it is explicitly taught (e.g., Laufer & Shmueli, 1997; Min, 2008; Zimmerman, 1997). Thus, if time is of the essence, as it is for most learners in secondary schools and college programs, explicit instruction is a necessary component in a writing course.

Vocabulary matters in writing, and students have weaker lexical proficiency. These two facts are irrefutable and need to be addressed through instruction. In other words, ESL writing teachers need to explicitly teach as much vocabulary as feasible—both early and often in our writing programs. Merely comprehending input or reading extensively will not suffice for the amount of vocabulary that a non-native speaker must learn to be able to compose well in English. Explicit instruction in specific vocabulary and in vocabulary learning strategies is essential.

2. Teach the right vocabulary from the right word list.

Your decision as to which vocabulary to teach should be based entirely on an analysis of your learners' writing needs. Why are the students in a writing class? Are your students attempting to pass an exam such as the TOEFL® or another institutional barrier exam? Are they preparing to enroll in a college or university where they will soon have to take a general composition course? Are they graduate students who have to write a research report or even a thesis? What will they read in your class? Do they have to write papers based on class lectures or in-class group interactions?

Once you have focused on student vocabulary needs, there may be a word list that approximates what your students need. I will discuss two older lists and two newer academic vocabulary lists. The older two are the University Word List (UWL) and the Academic Word List (AWL), while the more recent ones are the New Academic Word List (NAWL) and the Academic Spoken Word List (ASWL).

The University Word List (Xue & Nation, 1984) consists of 808 vocabulary words that are common in academic texts. Academic materials were used as the data source for the UWL because this list is designed to help learners who are in an academic setting—that is, those who want to study in high school, community college, or university.

The Academic Word List (Coxhead, 2000) consists of 570 word families (e.g., *commit, commitment, committed, committing*) that occurred in more than half of the 28 academic subject areas targeted in the corpus. The AWL came from an academic corpus of 3,500,000 words from which the word families were pulled to produce a list of academic words that are useful for the widest possible range of non-native learners of English.

The New Academic Word List (NAWL) (Gardner & Davies, 2014) comes from a corpus of 120 million words. I like this list because it identifies the specific member of a word family that is frequent and therefore more useful for your student. Instead of learning the word family for *profit* with *profit, profits, profited, profitable, unprofitable*, the NAWL would identify one form that is the most frequent and students could then focus their attention on that form instead of worrying about others.

It may seem strange that the next list included here deals with spoken language, but students sometimes have to include content from a class lecture or class discussions in their writing, even indirectly, so some students may also need help with spoken vocabulary that is frequent in academic settings. The Academic Spoken Word List (Dang et al., 2017) comes from a corpus of 13 million words. Like the AWL (Coxhead, 2000), it is based on word family.

For further information about academic word lists, see *Academic Word Lists: What Every Teacher Should Know* (Folse, 2020).

3. Encourage students to become vocabulary detectives.

While classroom vocabulary instruction is important, the number of unknown words is too great to be explicitly taught or even indirectly encountered in reading or listening within the very limited time frame that most learners have. To succeed, they must also become independent vocabulary learners, making use of the most efficient vocabulary learning strategies (Folse, 2020).

There is no magic list of best strategies that will guarantee success in learning vocabulary, and the most successful learners are those who have a very specific concrete plan of action and consistently carry it out (Folse, 2004; Sanaoui, 1995). One example of a concrete action that promotes vocabulary learning is keeping a **vocabulary notebook** (Folse, 2004, 2020; Hedgcock & Ferris, 2009).

A vocabulary notebook is only as valuable as the number of times learners actually refer to it to practice their words, so students should organize their notebooks based on their individual preferences, not their teacher's. I have heard from so many teachers who say they require their students to write the new word, its part of speech, and the complete definition from the dictionary, as well as an example sentence that might be given. In my opinion, this is too much information to copy for each word. With these instructions, adding 10 words to a notebook could easily take 30 minutes, which is far too long. In this scenario, the notebook becomes an assignment—a rather meaningless task—instead of a useful tool.

An entry for a word should be what the learner thinks is useful, not simply what the teacher thinks. (I would add here that many English teachers are monolinguals with little experience in attempting a new language, so I would yield to students with second language learning experiences here.) Most learners would like to add a translation into their native language, which research overwhelmingly supports (Folse, 2004; 2020). However, this practice is often frowned upon by ESL teachers (McCann, 2005). (For additional research that convincingly shows that translation is, in fact, effective in learning vocabulary, see Hulstijn, 1992, and Laufer & Girsai, 2008.)

Whether the teacher thinks using translations is an effective learning strategy or not is irrelevant for the student's notebook. The student's notebook belongs to the student. It is supposed to be a learning tool designed to help that student. If the student likes this strategy and feels comfortable with it, then that student is more likely to make more use of the notebook. This learner's initiative and hard work should be praised, not discouraged. Remember that our overall goal is to increase the frequency of interaction between the learner and the unknown vocabulary. A video of my own experience with a vocabulary notebook (or log) and the importance of it to each learner can be viewed here: https://www.youtube.com/watch?v=F8zacjvaYwc&t=52s.

Testing both passive and active vocabulary knowledge, Walters and Bozkurt (2009) found that learners who kept a vocabulary notebook learned significantly more vocabulary than similar learners in a control group that did not. Perhaps more important, those who kept a vocabulary notebook demonstrated a greater tendency to use the target words in freewriting compositions, thus improving the lexical profile of their writing.

When my students do freewriting assignments, I require them to use and underline two vocabulary items in their writing. Students must use one word that we recently studied and one unknown word from their dictionary or other source. I grade these short homework assignments based on the inclusion of the two underlined words (100), only one underlined word (50), or no underlined words (0). This activity challenges the status quo in which our learners continue to make do with the limited vocabulary they know and therefore never expand their lexical base. This simple assignment requires students to push their lexical limits. It also gets them more accustomed to taking responsibility for their vocabulary growth.

A word list can be excellent, but the word list alone will not suffice in meeting all your students' writing needs (Folse, 2020). The best strategy you can develop in your students is their ability to be aware of new vocabulary and to record new vocabulary items that they should then practice in their own writing.

For example, if your students want to write a paper for a psychology class, they must learn to become aware of, or notice, the vocabulary that is used in psychology writing. Texts of this genre often contain vocabulary such as *is concerned with*, *mental processes*, and *schools of thought*. Likewise, if your students want to learn to write reports of an original science experiment that they have conducted, they might need words such as *purpose*, *intensity*, and *precise data*.

Because our students have different academic goals in different fields, it should be clear that students must take the bulk of the responsibility to increase their vocabulary. Though explicit vocabulary instruction (from a book, a website, or a teacher) is an efficient way to learn vocabulary, the sheer volume of words to be learned demands that the learner be aggressive in identifying new words to learn. Yes, teachers should teach vocabulary, but our students' writing cannot progress quickly enough with new vocabulary lessons from the teachers alone. One strategy that students can use to learn vocabulary is to keep their own vocabulary list or notebook and to choose an organizational method that increases the likelihood that they will actually open their notebooks multiple times to review vocabulary. After the learners write the words in their notebooks, they can rewrite the words onto flashcards or they can type the words onto an online flashcard system such as Quizlet. The emphasis is not so much on how the student records the new words, but rather on just getting students to take responsibility for recording their own words.

4. Teach learners how to keep a vocabulary notebook that facilitates multiple retrievals of unknown or newly encountered vocabulary.

Keeping a vocabulary list or notebook is certainly one of the most effective and efficient techniques for students to assume the responsibility for learning vocabulary. However, it is imperative that students choose an organizational method that increases the likelihood that they will actually open their notebooks multiple times to review vocabulary. (See Folse, 2006b, for an empirically based discussion on the necessity of multiple retrievals in learning L2 vocabulary.) In reality, if learners do not review what they have written in their vocabulary notebooks multiple times, then the notebook is useless, and student time should be spent on another task.

Vocabulary notebooks can be formatted in many different ways. First, if students already have a system that works for them, they should definitely continue to follow that system. However, many students believe that a vocabulary notebook is a mere list of English words on the left, with a translation on the right. Translations are good, but this type of shallow list has limitations for multiple retrievals (Folse, 2020).

In *Vocabulary Myths* (Folse, 2004) and again in *Academic Word Lists* (Folse, 2020), I introduce a vocabulary notebook format with four pieces of information that allow four different ways to practice retrieval: with a synonym of the word, translation of the word from English to the L1, a translation of the L1 word to English, and a brief contextual example or collocation of the word. It is crucial that students lay out their vocabulary in a way that allows them to have those retrieval options.

In addition, this notebook should be inviting (e.g., with lots of white space), so there is a greater chance that learners will revisit the page to retrieve meaning or form of the new words. Figure 8.3 shows an example of notebook entries for three vocabulary words written by a Spanish-speaking ESL student who is in a first-year psychology class. Notice how the student has skipped a line (or lines) between vocabulary entries and clearly lined up the information in two distinct columns.

With this design, each of the four pieces of information about each entry is in the same place on the page: The translation is always in the top right

1. enhance	aumentar, acrecentar
improve, make greater	"X" can ________ self-esteem.
2. when it comes to "Y"	cuando se trata de "Y"
when you talk about "Y"	________ literacy, I think . . .

Figure 8.3 A Learner's Vocabulary Notebook for Multiple Retrievals

corner and the collocation always in the bottom right. Students can take a blank piece of paper, cut out one quarter of it, and slide the small open square up and down the notebook page, first with the open corner on the left and then on the right, to create four different practice questions. (See Folse, 2004, pp. 103–106, for a more thorough example and explanation of this technique.)

5. Teach collocations, not just single words.

The traditional notion that a word is the letters between the space before and after it (e.g., *cat, out, bright*) is misguided at best. Vocabulary encompasses much more, including idioms (e.g., *let the cat out of the bag*), phrasal verbs (e.g., *run out of* [*money, time, energy*]), and collocations (e.g., *a bright future, dire circumstances*).

While I believe that collocations are crucial to advanced writing, I want to make an especially strong case for the teaching of two specific categories of collocations: **adjective + noun collocations** (e.g., *different reason*) and **adverb of degree + past participle** as adjective + noun collocations (e.g., *widely known* or *widely known facts*).

First, collocations such as *bright future, negative impact*, and *empirical relationship* consist of a noun that is preceded by a specific adjective. In the case of *bright future*, we could substitute *good future* or *great future*, but neither pairing is as effective. In contrast, *bright future* sounds less like "basic ESL" and more like a combination that a native speaker might use in academic writing.

Second, collocations such as *internationally distributed, widely criticized*, and *significantly reduced rates* consist of an adverb of degree followed by a past participle used as an adjective, which may be a predicate adjective or an adjective preceding a noun. Compare these sentences:

Good: More people in Argentina read *El Clarín* than any other newspaper.
Better: The most widely read newspaper in Argentina is *El Clarín*.
Good: These products are distributed in many countries.
Better: These products are internationally distributed.

Helping students identify these collocations and learn them involves an acceptance by teachers that there is a strong link between academic reading and academic writing. In a two-step process, teachers should first train students to recognize or be sensitive to collocations in their academic reading material by, for example, asking students to underline whole phrases (as opposed to words only) that they may not know or may not understand well. Second, teachers should identify and explain the most useful and most frequently used collocations with the entire class. If students are keeping a vocabulary notebook, they should add these collocations to their list.

6. Test vocabulary. Hold learners accountable.

It is a well-known principle in education that learners tend to learn what is expected of them and usually—and unfortunately for teachers—not much more, so we must persuade students of the importance of vocabulary and then repeatedly hold them accountable for their vocabulary learning in class assessments.

What does "class assessments" mean? There are many possible forms, so choose the format that is best for your students and for yourself. Don't forget yourself! If you are teaching multiple classes per day with multiple preparations, then don't ask students to write original sentences with vocabulary.

Creating a test with the instructions *For each of the ten words given, write an original sentence that demonstrates you understand the meaning of the word* is easy to do. In fact, I just wrote half of your test for you. Now you only need to list the ten vocabulary words that your students studied in your class this week. While creating this test was quite simple and fast, scoring 10 sentences that 30 students have written means having to correct and comment on 300 sentences. While I am a very dedicated educator, this is probably too much work for one teacher, especially when you realize you need to give frequent vocabulary assessments. If you are not going to assess frequently, then don't bother to deal with vocabulary. If you are serious about trying to help your students, then include vocabulary in your quizzes or tests, and give these assessments frequently, maybe once a week if possible.

Rather than creating a test that requires so much grading time, why not use something that takes a little more time to create upfront but then is easier to score. In this way, you will save your overall time and be able to provide feedback to students a lot faster.

Here are some question formats that I would recommend:

Quiz 1. YES/NO

Is the underlined word used correctly?

1. _______ Maria did not want to do the work. She was feeling reveal.

Quiz 1 might look easy, but it is only easy for students if they know the word. In this section, you must resist the temptation to include grammar. This is vocabulary, so keep the focus of the question on vocabulary. One tip to writing these items is to write the sentence with the correct word and then substitute another target word for that word. In this example, the target word was *stubborn*. On the same list of words to learn was the word *reveal*, so I made a simple substitution. Now, you might be thinking that *reveal* is a verb and *stubborn* is an adjective, so they are not good to use in this question. However, the part of speech is only a real clue to students if they in fact know that information about each word. Therefore, this is a very good question to check if the students know the words.

Quiz 2. Multiple Fill in the Blanks.

Use two of the three words in the correct place in the sentence.

1. (*feedback, humorous, overall*) If you follow my advice, you'll save ______ ____ time and be able to provide __________ to your coworkers faster.

Everyone has given single fill-in-the blank quizzes where there are 10 sentences with 10 blanks and then 10 words in the word box to choose from. However, this item is much more demanding and allows you to test three target words in one sentence. It also more closely resembles writing because the sentence has multiple clauses instead of the usual single-clause subject-verb-object sentences typical of many fill-in-the-blank activities. This test item is very efficient in a writing class.

Quiz 3. Scrambled Sentence

Using all the words given, write a good sentence.

1. using schools instruction. to pandemic, are Due the online worldwide

The answer to Quiz 3 is *Due to the worldwide pandemic, schools are using online instruction.* Quiz 3 can be easy or difficult, depending on how many words and clauses are in your original sentence. Start with a real sentence that a student wrote in good paragraph or essay. Make sure that your item has only one answer, as this will facilitate faster grading. Avoid small adverbs of time such as *now* or *yesterday* because their position can vary in a sentence (*Now I'm hungry. I'm hungry now.*) and take longer to check and cause confusion when students want to know their errors. In addition, be careful that adjectives cannot vary in location. Here we have the adjectives *worldwide* and *online*. If students know the meaning of these two target words, then they should also know that *online pandemic* does not make sense and that *worldwide instruction* is possible theoretically but not here, given the instructions of having to use all the words in the sentence. On a final note, I decided to leave the capital letters and punctuation in, but some teachers may wish to omit these features to also test capitalization and punctuation. I think scrambled sentences can be a very good assessment instrument for vocabulary.

7. Teach paraphrasing and summarizing.

In courses ranging from remedial to graduate work, many academic writing assignments require students to read one or more original sources and then synthesize them into one original piece of writing. This process of synthesis is quite complex, involving sophisticated reading strategies and writing skills such as paraphrasing and summarizing.

In reading, vocabulary is essential: Not knowing even a handful of words can prevent comprehension. Next, students must paraphrase the key ideas, at least partially with another set of word and phrase synonyms to avoid plagiarism. Then students must be able to reduce the key paraphrased ideas to the most important points and then be able to weave the points from various sources—that is, to synthesize the ideas. While summarizing and synthesizing tend to have their own set of key vocabulary items (e.g., *on one hand, in conclusion, both*), reading comprehension and paraphrasing will require knowledge of an extremely large number of vocabulary items, including not only single words but also idioms, phrasal verbs, and collocations.

For further reading on paraphrasing and summarizing, including extensive examples of exercises practicing these two important writing skills, see *Great Writing 5: Greater Essays* (Folse & Pugh, 2020).

8. Make sure that explicit teaching of vocabulary is included in the writing program from the lowest levels of language proficiency.

Learning vocabulary in a second language is a daunting task because of the sheer quantity of single words, phrases, idioms, collocations, and other lexical chunks. In addition, learners must understand multiple aspects for each: its form and spelling, its pronunciation, its meaning(s), its connotations, its most common usages, and its register(s). All these aspects are even more complicated for L2 academic writing, so advanced writers need substantial repertoires of words, especially synonyms, nuanced connotations, and collocations—a huge task. The necessary time for the accumulation of such a vocabulary indicates that the study of basic academic vocabulary should begin early in the L2 learning process, not only in reading classes but in every ESL/EFL class, including writing.

Furthermore, research studies presented have shown that readers value the writer's words in their evaluation of the writer's message. Commonly used assessment rubrics often give substantial weight to vocabulary—either directly or indirectly—yet few English programs have a curriculum that explicitly and consistently addresses vocabulary. Unfortunately, ESL writing curricula continue to be dominated by grammar discussions.

In all my years of teaching in five countries, I have seen only one ESL program that included detailed vocabulary objectives, including which words to cover at a minimum. To be clear, I have seen many programs with nebulous learning objectives such as "Students will learn vocabulary appropriate for Level 3," or "Learners will be able to use advanced vocabulary for communication." However, these are superficial objectives that are often included, it seems, to occupy a space on a curriculum template.

One reason I have heard to explain why program objectives are often not very specific about lexical issues is that there are too many words to list. While there is some validity to this explanation, the same objectives will often go into great detail about ESL grammar.

Far too many programs have no real lexical goals for their students. A generic feel-good statement such as "Students will improve their vocabulary" is not a real objective. I want to be very clear here when I emphatically say that this is NOT a valid learning objective because it is not specific enough (Which vocabulary? For what purpose? For speaking? For writing?) and does not include how "improve" will be measured. How will everyone know when students have, in fact, improved their vocabulary?

If a program is not going to be specific about which vocabulary is to be covered in which courses, then the program should at least implement a program-wide policy regarding vocabulary instruction and assessment. For example, each teacher should have to identify 25 words or expressions to be taught each week, as well as how those lexical items will be practiced or assessed. At this point, most teachers and even some administrators may balk at 25 words per week, but this number is inconsequential to the number of lexical items that ESL students need if they are going to truly excel, not just exist, in a course that requires academic writing. In *Academic Word Lists* (Folse, 2020), I talk in some detail about the problem of setting a low lexical target. We should aim higher. The fact that not everyone achieves that high number does not mean should we not aim high.

With the low and sometimes non-existent lexical objectives I see in many programs today, it is not surprising that students' academic writing lacks lexical rigor. The solution is for all teachers, including writing teachers, to recognize the vocabulary gap that our students have and then implement specific lexical goals for all courses, including writing. Because of the important role that vocabulary plays in the success of academic writing, writing teachers should immediately make vocabulary an integral, not cursory, part of their daily classes.

• • •

In this volume, I have tried to explain the challenge our students—and teachers—face. Learning new vocabulary is not a simple step. Both teacher and students need to work toward vocabulary growth in their classes. Attaining the size and depth of vocabulary necessary to write well in an academic setting can be especially challenging. Learning each new word in a second language is rarely a simple yes/no proposition. Neither teachers nor students should equate knowing a word with a light switch that has only two options: on and off. Instead, we should think of a dimmer switch that can be cranked up (or down) in varying increments because learning vocabulary is a process.

To succeed in this lexical endeavor, teachers, administrators, and materials writers should reflect carefully. Is vocabulary explicitly covered in our teaching materials? Is vocabulary systematically covered in our courses? Do our writing rubrics address vocabulary? Are students in our writing classes keeping a vocabulary notebook that they use for multiple retrievals? Do teachers emphasize the importance of vocabulary through our teaching, our comments on student writing, and the questions we ask in our assessments? Only when we can answer yes to these questions will we demonstrate a true commitment to teaching vocabulary in our ESL/EFL writing courses.

QUESTIONS FOR REFLECTION

1. To what extent do you think that vocabulary in a given piece of writing influences a reader's perception of the quality of that piece of writing?
2. What do you think ESL writers believe about the role of vocabulary knowledge in the quality of their writing? Interview three ESL students to hear their opinions about vocabulary and their writing.
3. In composition/writing classes that you have taught (or observed), how extensively and systematically is vocabulary knowledge addressed?
4. How important is vocabulary in paraphrasing? Find a quote of three to five sentences from an expert on a current topic. Write a concise paraphrase of the original. Now notice which synonyms you used for which original words. Also, note which original words you did not include in the paraphrase. Remember that in order to know not to include them (because they are not important enough) you have to actually know those words, too. As a follow-up, give your task to a colleague and then compare their paraphrase with yours.
5. For further study and discussion, ask three native speakers and three non-native speakers to perform the task in Number 4. Compare the paraphrases in terms of vocabulary. Which group uses a better variety of synonyms? Which words or phrases were changed? Which were not changed? Were there some lexical items that non-native writers tended to do differently than the native writers?
6. Look at the curriculum for an upper-intermediate or advanced ESL writing class. Identify specific teaching objectives for: (a) composition (i.e., writing, editing, brainstorming, etc.), (b) grammar, and (c) vocabulary. How does the curriculum match or not match the information presented in this book? In particular, compare the amount of "book time" (e.g., paragraphs or pages) devoted to grammar relative to vocabulary. What message, if any, is being sent to students about these two areas within writing?

7. Good examples of composed, crafted writing can often be found in editorial columns in large news sources, journals, or blogs. Choose a selection from one of them to analyze. Can you identify collocations that make the writing sound appropriate for this venue? Are these collocations likely to be known by an NNS? Be sure to differentiate "known" in the passive sense (i.e., students can understand the collocation when they read it) from the active sense (i.e., students are able to retrieve this collocation from their English vocabulary knowledge and use it on their own).
8. Several teaching suggestions were made in Chapter 8, "What All Teachers Should Do," to help students improve the vocabulary used in their writing. Can you think of other concrete suggestions?

REFERENCES

Alderson, J. (1984). Reading in a foreign language: A reading problem or a language problem? In J. Alderson, & A. Urquhart (Eds.), *Reading in a foreign language* (pp. 1–27). London: Longman.

Alkhofi, A. (2015). Comparing the receptive vocabulary knowledge of intermediate-level students of different native languages in an intensive English program. *Electronic Theses and Dissertations, 2004–2019*, 48.

Ashrafzadeh, A., & Nimehchisalem, V. (2015). Vocabulary knowledge: Malaysian tertiary level learners' major problem in summary writing. *Journal of Language Teaching and Research, 6*(2), 286–291.

Atas, U. (2018). The role of receptive vocabulary knowledge in advanced EFL listening comprehension. *TESL-EJ, 2*(14), 1–11.

Baumann, J. F. (2009a). Intensity in vocabulary instruction and effects on reading comprehension. *Topics in Language Disorders, 29*(4), 312–328.

Baumann, J. F. (2009b). Vocabulary and reading comprehension: The nexus of meaning. In S. E. Israel & G. G. Duffy (Eds.), *Handbook of research on reading comprehension* (pp. 323–346). New York: Routledge.

Beck, I., Perfetti, C., & McKeown, M. (1982). Effects of text construction and instructional procedures for teaching word meanings on comprehension and recall. *Journal of Educational Psychology, 74*, 506–521.

Chen, M. (2019). Phrasal paraphrase learning: Exploring an effective strategy to consolidate vocabulary knowledge. *Taiwan Journal of TESOL, 16*(1), 41–66.

Choy, S., & Mun, L. (2012). Effects of teaching paraphrasing skills to students learning summary writing in ESL. *Journal of Teaching and Learning, 8*(2), 77–89.

Coady, J., Magoto, J., Hubbard, P., Graney, J., & Mokhtari, K. (1993). High frequency vocabulary and reading proficiency in ESL readers. In T. Huckin, M. Haynes, & J. Coady (Eds.), *Second language reading and vocabulary learning* (pp. 217–228). Norwood, NJ: Ablex.

Cobb, T. (1999). Breadth and depth of lexical acquisition with hands-on concordancing. *Computer Assisted Language Learning, 12*(4), 345–360.

Coxhead, A. (2000). A new academic word list. *TESOL Quarterly, 34*(2), 213–238.

Crusan, D. (2010). *Assessment in the second language writing classroom.* Ann Arbor: University of Michigan Press.

Daller, H., van Hout, R., & Treffers-Daller, J. (2003). Lexical richness in the spontaneous speech of bilinguals. *Applied Linguistics, 24*, 197–222.

Dang, T., Coxhead, A., & Webb, S. (2017). An academic spoken word list. *Language Learning, 67*(4), 959–997.

Dordick, M. (1996). Testing for a hierarchy of the communicative interference of errors. *System, 24*(3), 299–308.

Educational Testing Service (2019). Performance descriptors for the TOEFL iBT® test. Retrieved from https://www.ets.org/s/toefl/pdf/pd-toefl-ibt.pdf

Educational Testing Service (2019). Understanding your TOEFL iBT® scores. Retrieved from https://www.ets.org/toefl/test-takers/ibt/scores/unders tanding

Ellis, R., Tanaka, Y., & Yamazaki, A. (1994). Classroom interaction, comprehension, and the acquisition of L2 word meanings. *Language Learning, 44*, 449–491.

Engber, C. (1995). The relationship of lexical proficiency to the quality of ESL compositions. *Journal of Second Language Writing, 4*(2), 139–155.

Ferris, D. (1994). Lexical and syntactic features of ESL writing by students at different levels of L2 proficiency. *TESOL Quarterly, 28*(2), 414–420.

Ferris, D. (2018). *What error correction can(not) accomplish for second language writers: Dispelling myths, discussing options.* Ann Arbor: University of Michigan Press.

Flesch, R. (1955). *Why Johnny can't read.* New York: Harper Brothers.

Folse, K. (2004). *Vocabulary myths: Applying second language research to classroom teaching.* Ann Arbor: University of Michigan Press.

Folse, K. (2006a). *The art of teaching speaking: Research and pedagogy for the ESL/EFL classroom.* Ann Arbor: University of Michigan Press.

Folse, K. (2006b). The effect of type of written exercise on L2 vocabulary retention. *TESOL Quarterly, 40*(2), 273–293.

Folse, K. (2020). *Academic word lists: What every teacher needs to know.* Ann Arbor: University of Michigan Press.

Folse, K., & Pugh, T. (2020). *Great Writing 5: Greater Essays (From Essays to Research).* Boston, MA: National Geographic Learning.

Gardner, D., & Davies, M. (2014). A new academic vocabulary list. *Applied Linguistics, 35*(3), 305–327.

González, M. (2017). The contribution of lexical diversity to college-level writing. *TESOL Journal, 8*, 899–919.

Green, D., & Meara, P. (1995). Guest editorial. *Computer Assisted Language Learning, 8*(2–3), 97–101.

Haynes, M. (1993). Patterns and perils of guessing in second language reading. In T. Huckin, M. Haynes, & J. Coady (Eds.), *Second language reading and vocabulary learning* (pp. 46–64). Norwood, NJ: Ablex.

Hedgcock, J., & Ferris, D. (2009). *Teaching readers of English: Students, texts, contexts.* New York: Routledge.

Hilton, H. 2008. The link between vocabulary knowledge and spoken L2 fluency. *Language Learning Journal, 36*(2), 153–166.

Hu, M., & Nation, P. (2000). Vocabulary density and reading comprehension. *Reading in a Foreign Language, 13*(1), 403–430.

Huckin, T., & Bloch, J. (1993). Strategies for inferring word meaning in context: A cognitive model. In T. Huckin, M. Haynes, & J. Coady (Eds.), *Second language reading and vocabulary acquisition* (pp. 153–178). Norwood, NJ: Ablex.

Hulstijn, J. (1992). Retention of inferred and given word meanings: Experiments in incidental vocabulary learning. In P. Arnaud & H. Bejoint (Eds.), *Vocabulary and applied linguistics* (pp. 113–125). London: Macmillan.

Hyland, K., & Hyland, F. (2006). Feedback on second language students' writing. *Language Teaching, 39*, 83–101.

Jacobs, H., Hartfiel, V., Hughey, J., & Wormuth, D. (1981). *Testing ESL composition: A practical approach.* Boston, MA: Newbury House.

James, M. (1996). Improving second language reading comprehension: A computer-assisted vocabulary development approach. Ph.D. diss. University of Hawaii, Manoa.

Joe, A. (1995). Text-based tasks and incidental vocabulary learning: A case study. *Second Language Research, 11*(2), 159–177.

Joe, A., Nation, P., & Newton, J. (1996). Vocabulary learning and speaking activities. *English Teaching Forum, 34*(1), 2–7.

Kameenui, E., Carnine, D., & Freschi, R. (1982). Effects of text construction and instructional procedures for teaching word meanings on comprehension and recall. *Reading Research Quarterly, 17*, 367–388.

Koizumi, R., & In'nami, Y. (2013). Vocabulary knowledge and speaking proficiency among second language learners from novice to intermediate levels. *Journal of Language Teaching and Research, 4*(5), 900–913.

Laufer, B. (1992). How much lexis is necessary for reading comprehension? In P. Arnaud & H. Bejoint (Eds.), *Vocabulary and applied linguistics.* London: Macmillan.

Laufer, B. (1994). Appropriation du vocabulaire: Mots faciles, mots difficiles, mots impossibles. *Acquisition et Interaction en Langue Etrangére*, 3, 97–113.

Laufer, B. (1997). The lexical plight in second language reading: Words you don't know, words you think you know, and words you can't guess. In J. Coady & T. Huckin (Eds.), *Second language vocabulary acquisition* (pp. 20–34). Cambridge, England: Cambridge University Press.

Laufer, B., & Girsai, N. (2008). Form-focused instruction in second language vocabulary learning: A case for contrastive analysis and translation. *Applied Linguistics, 29*, 694–716.

Laufer, B., & Nation, P. (1995). Vocabulary size and use: Lexical richness in L2 written production. *Applied Linguistics, 16*(3), 307–322.

Laufer, B., & Ravenhorst-Kalovski, G. (2010). Lexical threshold revisited: Lexical coverage, learners' vocabulary size and reading comprehension. Reading in a Foreign *Language, 22*(1), 15–30.

Laufer, B., & Shmueli, K. (1997). Memorizing new words: Does teaching have anything to do with it? *RELC Journal, 28*(1), 89–108.

Laufer, B., & Yano, Y. (2001). Understanding unfamiliar words in a text: Do L2 learners understand how much they don't understand? *Reading in a Foreign Language, 13*, 549–566.

Leki, I., & Carson, J. (1994). Students' perceptions of EAP writing instruction and writing needs across the disciplines. *TESOL Quarterly, 28*, 81–101.

Lennon, P. (1996). Getting "easy" verbs wrong at the advanced level. *International Review of Applied Linguistics, 34*(1), 23–36.

Linnarud, M. (1986). Lexis in composition: A performance analysis of Swedish learners' written English. *Lund Studies in English, 74*.

Llach, M. (2005). The relationship of lexical error and their types to the quality of ESL compositions: An empirical study. *Porta Linguarum: International Magazine for the Teaching of German, 3*, 45–57.

Matthews, J., & Cheng, J. (2015). Recognition of high frequency words from speech as a predictor of L2 listening comprehension. *System, 52*, 1–13.

McCann, K. (2005). Not lost in translation. *IATEFL Issues, 186*, 8.

McNamara, D., Crossley, S., & McCarthy, P. (2010). Linguistic features of writing quality. *Written Communication, 27*(1), 57–86.

Meara, P. (1980). Vocabulary acquisition: A neglected aspect of language learning. *Language Teaching and Linguistics: Abstracts, 13*(4), 221–246.

Mecartty, F. (2000). Lexical and grammatical knowledge in reading and listening comprehension by foreign language learners of Spanish. *Applied Language Learning, 11*, 323–348.

Mehrpour, S., & Rahimi, M. (2010). The impact of general and specific vocabulary knowledge on reading and listening comprehension: A case of Iranian EFL learners. *System, 38*(2), 292–300.

Min, H. (2008). EFL vocabulary acquisition and retention: Reading plus vocabulary enhancement activities and narrow reading. *Language Learning, 58*(1), 73–115.

Na, C., & Nhat, N. (2017). Paraphrasing in academic writing: A case study of Vietnamese learners of English. *Language Education in Asia, 8*(1), 9–24.

Nation, P. (1983). Testing and teaching vocabulary. *Guidelines*, 5(1), 12–25.

Nation, P., & Coady, J. (1988). Vocabulary and reading. In R. Carter & M. McCarthy (Eds.), *Vocabulary learning and teaching* (pp. 97–110). London: Longman.

Newton, J. (1995). Task-based interaction and incidental vocabulary learning: A case study. *Second Language Research, 11*, 159–177.

Peters, E., & Webb, S. (2018). Incidental vocabulary acquisition through viewing L2 television and factors that affect learning. *Studies in Second Language Acquisition, 40*, 551–577.

Pica, T. (1994). Research on negotiation: What does it reveal about second-language learning conditions, processes, and outcomes? *Language Learning, 44*, 493–527.

Pigada, M., & Schmitt, N. (2006). Vocabulary acquisition from extensive reading: A case study. *Reading in a Foreign Language, 18*, 1–28.

Pizarro, M. (2003). A study of different composition elements that raters respond to. Estudios Ingleses de la *Universidad Complutense, 11*, 53–72.

Qian, D. (2002). Investigating the relationship between vocabulary knowledge and academic reading performance: An assessment perspective. *Language Learning, 52*(3), 513–536.

Read, J. (1998). Validating a test to measure depth of vocabulary knowledge. In A. Kunnan (Ed.), *Validation in language assessment* (pp. 41–60). Mahwah, NJ: Erlbaum.

Reid, J. (Ed.) (2008). *Writing myths: Applying second language Research to classroom teaching.* Ann Arbor: University of Michigan Press.

Roberts, F., & Cimasko, T. (2008). Evaluating ESL: Making sense of university professors' responses to second language writing. *Journal of Second Language Writing*, *17*, 125–143.

Ruegg, R., Fritz., E., & Holland, J. (2011). Rater sensitivity to qualities of lexis in writing. *TESOL Quarterly*, *45*, 63–80.

Sanaoui, R. (1995). Adult learners' approaches to learning vocabulary in second languages. *Modern Language Journal*, *79*(1), 15–28.

Santos, T. (1988). Professors' reactions to the academic writing of non-native-speaking students. *TESOL Quarterly*, *22*(1), 69–90.

Schmitt, N., & Schmitt, D. (2014). A reassessment of frequency and vocabulary size in L2 vocabulary teaching. *Language Teaching*, *47*(4), 484–503. DOI:10.1017/S0261444812000018.

Solanò, A. (2014). Vocabulary in speaking performance, research report for master in English language teaching. Unpublished thesis, Universidad de La Sabana, Colombia.

Stæhr, L. (2009). Vocabulary knowledge and advanced listening comprehension in English as a foreign language. *Studies in Second Language Acquisition*, *31*(4), 577–607.

Straub, R. (1997). Students' reactions to teacher comments: An exploratory study. *Research in the Teaching of English*, *31*(1), 91–119.

Tsui, A., & Ng. M. (2000). Do secondary L2 writers benefit from peer comments? *Journal of Second Language Writing*, *9*(2), 147–170.

Walters, J., & Bozkurt, N. (2009). The effect of keeping vocabulary notebooks on vocabulary acquisition. *Language Teaching Research*, *13*, 403–423.

Wilkins, D. (1972). *Linguistics in language teaching*. London: Arnold.

Xue, G., & Nation, I. S. P. (1984). A university word list. *Language Learning and Communication*, *3*(2), 215–229.

Zimmerman, C. (1997). Do reading and interactive vocabulary instruction make a difference? An empirical study. *TESOL Quarterly*, *31*, 121–140.